Ariana Grande · Sweetener

ISBN: 978-1-5400-3780-0

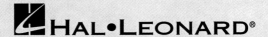

Visit Hal Leonard Online at
www.halleonard.com

Contact us:
Hal Leonard
7777 West Bluemound Road
Milwaukee, WI 53213
Email: info@halleonard.com

In Europe, contact:
Hal Leonard Europe Limited
42 Wigmore Street
Marylebone, London, W1U 2RN
Email: info@halleonardeurope.com

In Australia, contact:
Hal Leonard Australia Pty. Ltd.
4 Lentara Court
Cheltenham, Victoria, 3192 Australia
Email: info@halleonard.com.au

AN ANGEL CRIED

Words and Music by
BOB GAUDIO

Moderately, in 2

N.C.

When rain-drops fell down from the sky, the day you left me, an an-gel cried.

Oh, she cried. An an-gel cried, she cried.

(L.H. tacet throughout)

THE LIGHT IS COMING

Words and Music by ARIANA GRANDE,
ONIKA MARAJ and PHARRELL WILLIAMS

Urban beat

Ay yo, tro-phy wife, out __ you won me un - til you had to find out __ it's one me.

Now you benched, aww, __ your bum knee. Now I'm the bad guy, call __ me Chun - Li.

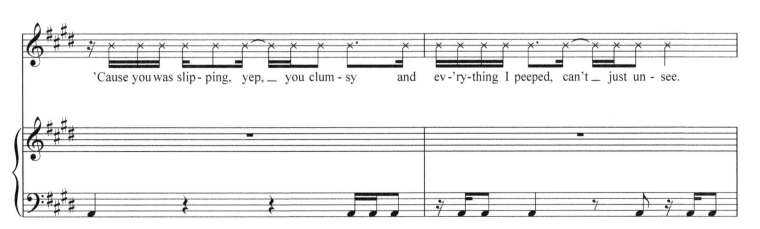

'Cause you was slip-ping, yep, __ you clum-sy and ev-'ry-thing I peeped, can't __ just un - see.

Sips tea and __ it's un-sweet. With re - spect bad girl, when __ me done, speak. Now,

now, now he shoot-ing his shot __ like drive by. Why you had to make me go call up my side guy?

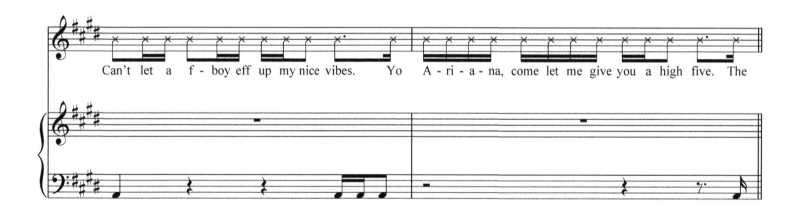

Can't let a f - boy eff up my nice vibes. Yo A - ri - a - na, come let me give you a high five. The

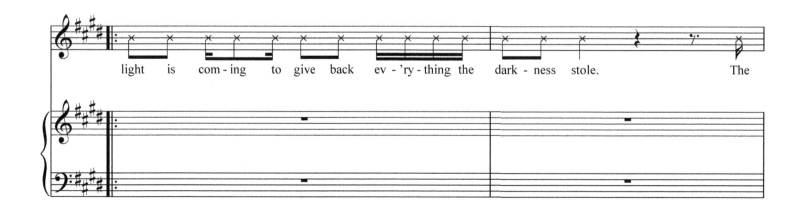

light is com-ing to give back ev - 'ry - thing the dark - ness stole. The

glow at all. __ (Glow at all.) __ Know it all. __ (Know it all.) __ The

N.C.

light is com-ing to give back ev-'ry-thing the dark - ness stole. The

light is com-ing to give back ev-'ry-thing the dark - ness stole. The

light is com-ing to give back ev-'ry-thing the dark - ness stole. The

BLAZED

Words and Music by ARIANA GRANDE,
MAXINE COLON and PHARRELL WILLIAMS

Moderate Pop

There is some-thing be-tween us, I can see ___ it right

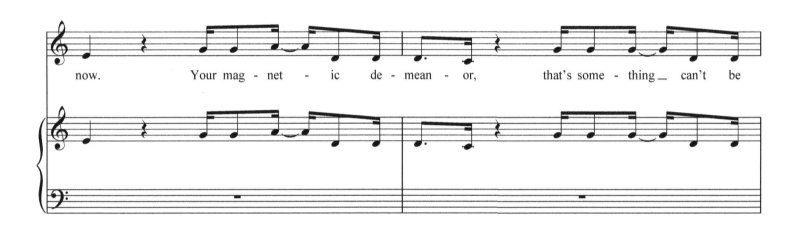

now. Your mag-net-ic de-mean-or, that's some-thing ___ can't be

found. I thought that I ___ was dream-ing 'til my love ___ came a-

R.E.M.

Words and Music by ARIANA GRANDE
and PHARRELL WILLIAMS

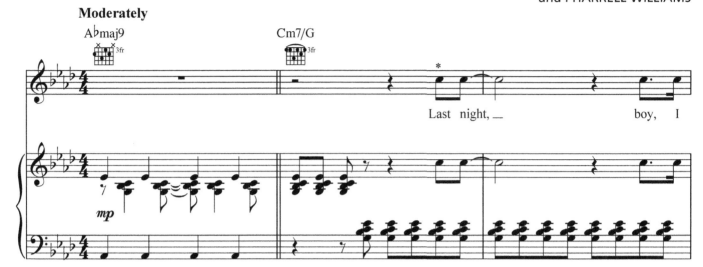

*Lead vocal sung an octave lower than written.

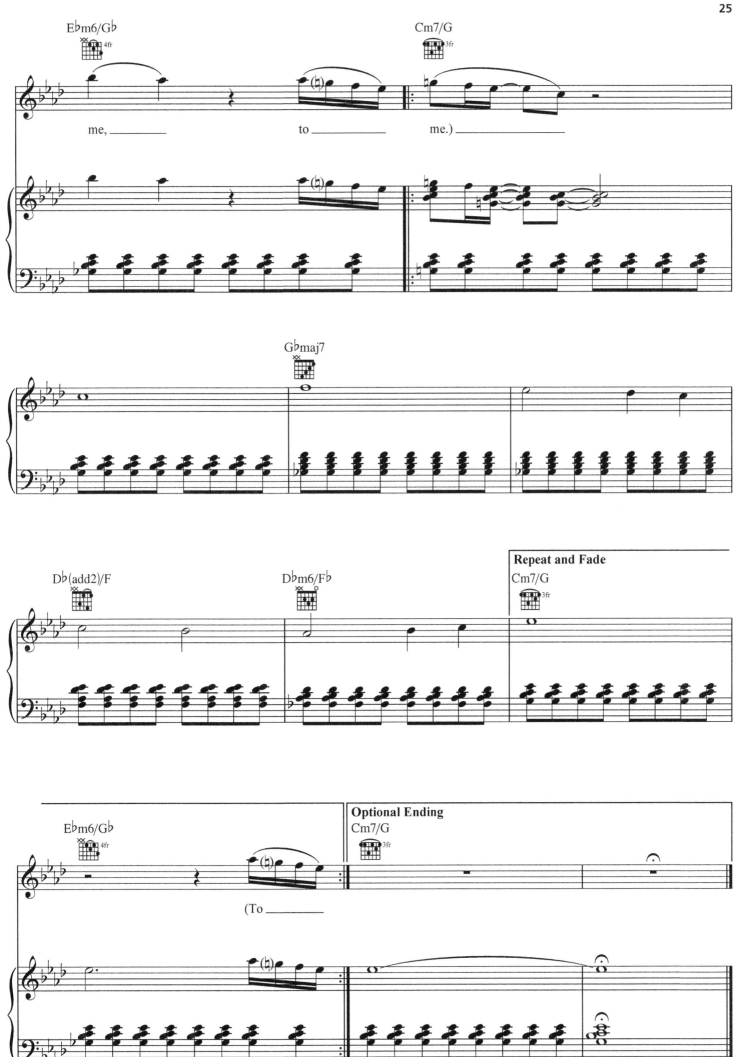

GOD IS A WOMAN

Words and Music by ARIANA GRANDE,
RICHARD GORANSSON, MAX MERTIN,
SAVAN KOTECHA and ILYA

SWEETENER

Words and Music by ARIANA GRANDE
and PHARRELL WILLIAMS

Moderately fast

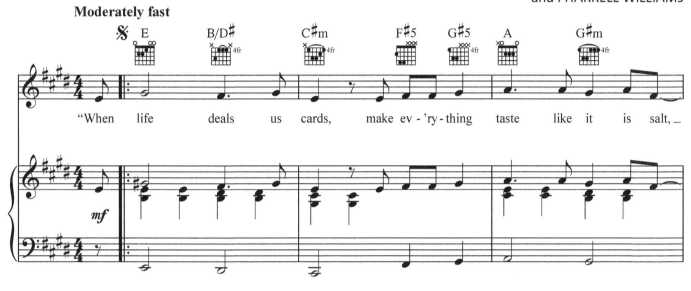

"When life deals us cards, make ev - 'ry-thing taste like it is salt, __

__ then you come through like the sweet - 'ner you are to bring the

bit - ter taste to a halt." __ And then you get it, get it, get it, get it,

SUCCESSFUL

Words and Music by ARIANA GRANDE
and PHARRELL WILLIAMS

I just got some real good news from work, boy. (It's a sur- prise, a sur- prise.) You can't im- ag- ine

To Coda

EVERYTIME

Words and Music by ARIANA GRANDE,
SAVAN KOTECHA, MAX MARTIN
and ILYA

Recorded a half-step lower

D.S. al Coda

They keep call-ing me a head case 'cause I can't make a good case why we can't change. I've

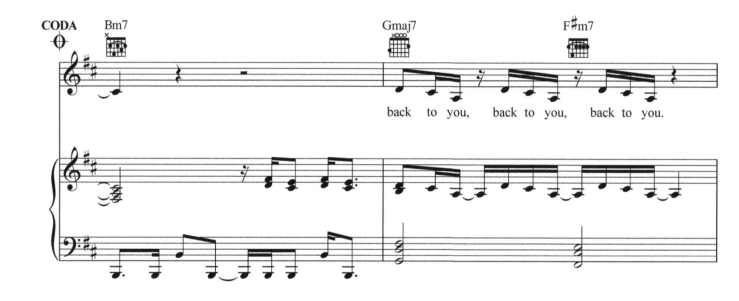

CODA

back to you, back to you, back to you.

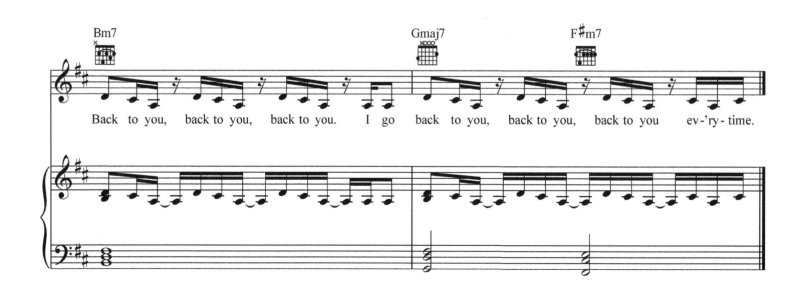

Back to you, back to you, back to you. I go back to you, back to you, back to you ev-'ry-time.

BREATHIN

Words and Music by ARIANA GRANDE,
SAVAN KOTECHA, MAX MARTIN and ILYA

NO TEARS LEFT TO CRY

Words and Music by ARIANA GRANDE,
SAVAN KOTECHA, MAX MARTIN
and ILYA

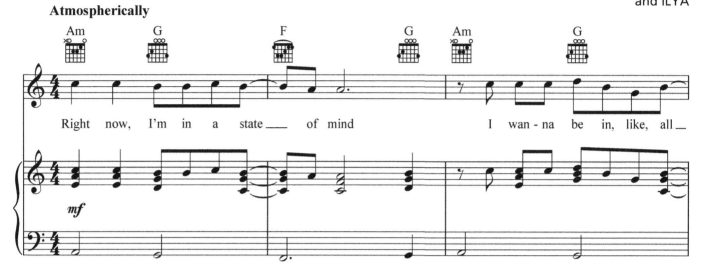

PETE DAVIDSON

Words and Music by ARIANA GRANDE,
CHARLES ANDERSON, THOMAS BROWN
and VICTORIA McCANTS

*Recorded a half step higher.

BORDERLINE

Words and Music by ARIANA GRANDE,
PHARRELL WILLIAMS and MISSY ELLIOT

BETTER OFF

Words and Music by ARIANA GRANDE,
CHAUNCEY HOLLIS, BRIAN BAPTISTE,
TOMMY BROWN and KIMBERLY KRYSIUK

Moderate Ballad

No, ___ no, ___ no, ___ no.

No, ___ no, ___ no. ___ No, ___ no, ___ no, ___ no.

You keep me in

* Recorded a half-step lower

Cmaj7
Fmaj7
Steer-ing clear of an-y head-aches to start. And if we're be-ing hon - est, I'd
Cmaj7
Fmaj7
rath-er your bod-y than half of your heart. Or jeal-ous rid-den com - ments that
Cmaj7
Fmaj7
come when you let in them feel-ings that I don't want. I nev-er let them
Dm
G
know too much, hate get-ting too e - mo - tion - al, yeah.

GOODNIGHT N GO

Words and Music by ARIANA GRANDE,
IMOGEN HEAP, TOMMY BROWN,
CHARLES ANDERSON, M. FOSTER
and VICTORIA McCANTS

GET WELL SOON

Words and Music by ARIANA GRANDE
and PHARRELL WILLIAMS

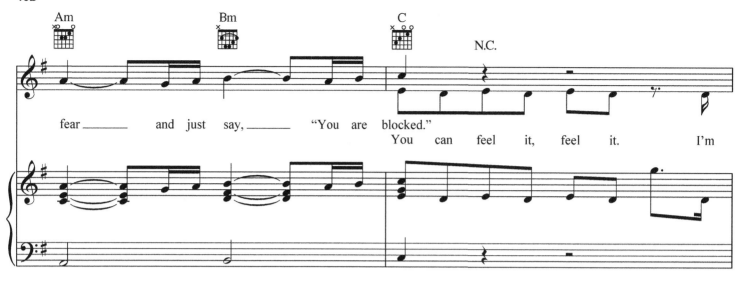

fear _____ and just say, _____ "You are blocked." You can feel it, feel it. I'm

with you, I'm with you, I'm with you, just call me, I'm with you, I'm with you. Just know there

is _____ so much room _____ at the top. You can feel it, feel it. I'm

with you, I'm with you, I'm with you, just call me, no mat-ter the is-sue.

Spoken: *"No matter what."*

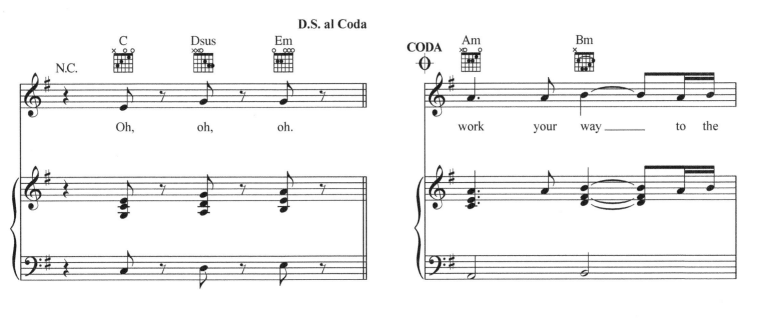

D.S. al Coda

Oh, oh, oh.

CODA

work your way _____ to the

top. You can feel it, feel it.